BASKETBALL 2

By Mark Littleton

ZondervanPublishingHouse
Grand Rapids, Michigan

A Division of HarperCollins*Publishers*

Basketball 2
Copyright © 1996 by Mark Littleton

Requests for information should be addressed to:

▤ ZondervanPublishingHouse
Grand Rapids, Michigan 49530

Library of Congress Cataloging-in-Publication Data

Littleton, Mark R., 1950–
    Basketball 2 / Mark Littleton.
      p. cm. — (Sports heroes)
    Includes bibliographical references.
    Summary: Life stories of eight players known for their Christian values
as well as for their skill at basketball.
    ISBN: 0-310-20265-5 (softcover)
    1. Basketball players—United States—Biography—Juvenile literature.
2. Basketball players—United States—Religious life—Juvenile literature.
[1. Basketball players. 2. Christian life.] I. Title. II. Series: Littleton,
Mark R., 1950–   Sports heroes.
GV884.A1L59   1996
796.357'092'2—dc20   96-14467
[B]   CIP
                                           AC

Edited by Tom Raabe
Interior design by Joe Vriend

Printed in the United States of America

96 97 98 99 00 01 02 / ❖ DH/ 10 9 8 7 6 5 4 3 2 1

To Jeff and Judy Winter,
who remain the best friends
anyone could ask for.

Contents

Playing with Commitment

Here we go again! More basketball greats from the halls of the National Basketball Association (NBA).

Take a good look at these eight players. Learn. Grow. Marvel. Praise. And thank God for their work, their testimony, and their commitment to Christian truth.

These men are not only great basketball players, but great Christians and great people too. We can imitate their play on the court, but their walk with the Lord of heaven is what remains after all the games are played.

Each one of them believes a gospel that is available to all of us. What is that gospel? Jesus died for our sins, and he rose again on the third day. Believe and you shall live.

Do you believe that?

I hope so. But if not, start today.

So read on with joy, and read with faith in your heart. God can use you too. And maybe one day you'll be a sports hero to a young Christian guy just like yourself.

Mark Littleton
August 1995

Chapter 1

☆ Julius Erving ☆

Height: 6 feet, 7 inches

Weight: 210 pounds

Position: Forward

Birth date: February 22, 1950

Team: **Philadelphia 76ers**

Julius Erving: Dr. J

Give the ball to Dr. J!" someone shouts from the stands.

The 76ers have the ball. There's a pass to Jones. He dribbles it and fires a through-the-legs pass to Toney. Toney pumps. He fakes. Now he passes. Malone has it in the key. He dips, slides, dribbles. A behind-the-back pass—

"Give it to Dr. J!" more people shout.

Dr. J—Julius Erving—is running some of his patented patterns, through the key, out to the stump, back, around.

Suddenly, the ball is in his hands.

"Go, Doc!"

"Hit one, Dr. J!"

"Dunk it!"

There's a gap in the defense. Dr. J dribbles. He leaps and spins, swiveling the ball from left to right to left again. The great hands come down, but he's still in the air.

Slam!

Two points!

"He did it! He did it!"

And he would do it again and again. Over his fifteen-year career he'd do it to the tune of 30,026 lifetime points, both in the now extinct American Basketball Association (ABA) and in the NBA.

Some say he's the greatest all-round basketball player of all time. Better than Magic Johnson. Better than Wilt Chamberlain. Better than Kareem Abdul-Jabbar, too. And maybe even Michael Jordan.

Maybe.

Julius Erving is a naturally humble guy. He doesn't make any claims to fame. He just went out, did his job, helped the team, and worked together with the other guys. Though individually he is an all-time great, he is the ultimate great team player.

Just how great? Well, read on.

Julius Erving started life in Hampstead, New York. His mother, Callie Mae Lindsey, was the daughter of South Carolina sharecroppers. She had thirteen sisters and brothers, and loved kids. But by the time Julius was five, his father had left the family. Julius stayed with his mother, an older sister named Alexis and a younger brother named Marvin. There was plenty of love in that little family.

Mrs. Lindsey gave Julius some freedom, and he spent it on the basketball courts in his hometown of Roosevelt, New York. There he learned the playground moves that would characterize his style in later years. Still, he would shy away from the flashy, "watch-me" style that many youngsters develop. He played for the team and made winning games a group effort. He didn't want all the glory for himself.

It was in sixth grade that Julius got the nickname Doctor. One of his teachers wanted to impress on him the possibility of becoming a professional—a doctor, lawyer, or teacher—when he grew up. So the teacher started calling him "Doctor." So did his friends.

But it was basketball, not medicine, that called to Julius. His junior high school coaches recognized his talent right away. And when he went on to set some marks as a six-foot-three-inch forward at Roosevelt High School, the colleges came calling. He had so many scholarship offers it took him days just to sift through the letters. Finally, he settled on the University of Massachusetts. At U Mass Julius could remain close to home and at the same time attend a good school.

In college the Doctor excelled on the court as no one had before him. He became the ultimate all-round player. He rebounded with one hand—his hands are larger than seven-foot-two-inch Kareem Abdul-Jabbar's. He learned to pass and shoot from almost any position—standing, dribbling, running, crouching, lying on the floor! And his gravity-defying, rim-ripping dunks were a marvel to behold. He seemed to hang weightless in the air. Starting from just past the free-throw line, he could leap, spin, switch hands, and dunk—all in one swift motion.

While at U Mass, Julius played 52 games, scored 1,370 points, and averaged 26.3 points a game. But a tragedy during his freshman year set a tone that Julius couldn't forget for years afterward. His mother and his brother Marvin, whom Julius believed could become a lawyer or doctor, drove up to Amherst to see Julius play. On the way home, Marvin complained of pain in his legs and arms. After putting him through tests in a hospital, the doctors thought it was arthritis. When Julius came home for spring break, Marvin remained in bed. After Julius returned to U Mass, his mother called with bad news. Marvin had died.

The doctors discovered he had a rare disease—lupus erythematosus—that produces deadly antibodies in the blood. The result is that the blood literally poisons itself.

Julius was badly shaken. His brother's death made him realize, for the first time in his life, that he couldn't control things. He couldn't will things to turn out for his family, or for himself. At that point he decided to live a clean, pure life, to do his best to be a good person. It wasn't a religious conversion, but the Doctor was thinking he had some serious living to do.

After two stellar years at U Mass, the pros came calling. Eventually, the Virginia Squires of the ABA offered Julius a $500,000 contract for four years. It was the most money he'd ever seen in his life. He had a hard decision to make: remain at U Mass for his senior year, or turn pro.

He turned pro. Immediately he sent some of that money home to help his mother and sister. And he burned up the court with the Squires. He averaged 27 points a game and was named ABA Rookie of the Year.

It was with the Squires that the Doctor unveiled his supreme move: the show-stopping dunk. In addition to your basic stuff-it-in-the-basket, straight-on dunk, Doctor J had a multitude of other slams: a dunk after catching a pass with one hand; a dunk behind his head; a dunk while cycling his legs in the air; a dunk with a spin; a dunk with two spins; a dunk off a blocked shot; a dunk and a hang on the rim.

You name it, he did it. He brought all the classic New York playground moves into the arena.

Why hadn't he done this in college? Because at that time you weren't allowed to dunk in college! Colleges played under the "Lew Alcindor" rule, named after Kareem Abdul-Jabbar (Lew Alcindor was his original name), which prohibited dunking. So when Julius appeared on the scene in the ABA, he brought an explosion of dunk shots with him that he'd been itching to use for three years. His second season with the Squires, he scored an average of 31.9 points a game, the highest in the league. He made the ABA all-star team his first two years.

His third year in the ABA, Dr. J hit pay dirt. He was traded to the New York Nets and won a brand new deal: $2.5 million for eight years, an incredible sum in 1973. People began coming to games specifically to see Dr. J play. It was the beginning years of the superstars, and Dr. J, already a well-known and popular player, was number one on the block. Not only was he a good player, he was also an entertainer. His flashy moves, his smooth, gravity-defying dunks, his one-on-one mastery—all of it contributed to making him the number one all-round player to watch.

In his three years with the Nets, Dr. J led them to two ABA championships (in 1974 and 1976) and won both most valuable player (MVP) in the league and MVP in the finals. In his first year with the Nets, he led the league in scoring, was third in blocked shots, third in steals, sixth in assists, seventh in rebounding, and ninth in field-goal accuracy. He was the all-round player par excellence. In one game against San Diego he scored 63 points. In the first game of the 1974 ABA Final against the Utah Stars, Julius scored 47 points, more than half of his team's total of 89.

Game three of those finals was one to remember. With less than eight minutes to go in the fourth quarter the Nets were ahead by 15 points. But the Stars went on a roll and racked up 18 points to take a three-point lead. The coach called for a three-point shot from Julius, but somehow Dr. J never got the ball. Somebody else took the shot—and missed it. But the Nets rebounded, and another player, Wendell Ladner, ended up with the ball just outside the three-point line. He fired. Zing. Three points. Tie game. The Nets went on a bender after that and ended up winning, 103–100.

The Nets lost the fourth game, but came back and won the fifth, capturing the championship. It was just the kind of excitement the league needed. The

Nets were on top, and Julius Erving was at the top of his game.

The accolades came pouring in. A teammate said, "Sometimes I watch Julius do something that I know I'll never see again on a basketball floor. He's a legend in his own time."[1]

One writer described Dr. J this way: "He's got all the moves of Earl Monroe, except Monroe does them on the ground and Julius does them in the air."[2]

Julius himself said, "I like to think I can do anything anyone else can do. And a few things others can't do, too. It's part of the completeness I've desired as a player."[3]

By the time the ABA was ready to fold, Julius had scored 11,662 points. He averaged 28.7 points per game, played on five all-star teams, and had been named MVP twice. In the 1976 finals, he led the Nets to a 4–2 win in games over the Denver Nuggets. Julius scored 45, 48, 31, 34, 37, and 31 points in those six games, in that order. He was ready for the NBA. And the NBA needed him.

The ABA's fortunes had gone sour by 1976, and the team owners decided to fold it up. Some said it was Dr. J alone who made possible the merger. His razzle-dazzle play was a crowd pleaser, and more and more people were coming just to see him play. Dick Motta, a veteran NBA coach, said, "Erving was the key element in professional basketball's resurgence. Julius saved the league."[4]

Dave DeBusschere, ABA commissioner, said, "Plenty of guys have been 'The Franchise.' For us, Dr. J is 'The League.'"[5]

Four teams from the ABA, including the Nets, were absorbed into the NBA. But the Nets were cash-poor. They needed money, and they needed to rebuild. They decided to deal Dr. J to the Philadelphia 76ers.

On his new team, Dr. J found himself just one among several major stars. With the Nets, he had been the go-to guy. Now he was one of several go-to guys. His scoring average dropped from 29 points a game to 21. Some commentators began to criticize.

The next season was worse. Julius suffered some injuries and didn't play for several games. His shooting was off and he was not the star attraction he'd been with the Nets. Even his dunks seemed to drool a little. It was then that Julius did some new thinking.

"At age twenty-nine I realized I was looking good on the outside," he said, "but was hitting a lot of peaks and valleys on the inside. After searching for the meaning of life for over ten years, I found meaning in Jesus Christ.

"When I gave my life to Jesus Christ I began to understand my true purpose for being here. It's not to go through life and experience as many things as you possibly can and then turn to dust and be no more. The purpose of life is to be found through having Christ in your life, understanding what his plan is, and following that plan.

"Since I asked Christ to be my Lord and Savior, there are still some peaks and valleys. But I am operated on by the greatest Doctor of them all."[6]

Julius's conversion brought a new attitude. He had been an ABA star, an all-star, and had led his team to two championships. In the NBA he'd been on the all-star team his first two years (in fact, he would play on it every year he played in the NBA). But the 76ers were not even looking like contenders, let alone champions.

Times were changing, though, and things began to look better. Julius's new way of thinking, his commitment to Christ, and his desire to be a truly good and decent guy were paying off.

In 1980, the 76ers made it to the finals, but lost to the Lakers, 4–2. In 1981, the 76ers lost the Eastern Conference Championship to the Celtics. Julius was voted MVP of the league, though, a real high.

Then in 1982, the 76ers beat the Celtics for the Eastern Conference title. They lost, though, to the Lakers, 4–2, in the finals. Julius was looking to 1983 for a big year.

It was. Philadelphia went on a huge roll the whole season. They were unstoppable. They clobbered the opposition that season, 65–17, under Dr. J's leadership and drive. The dunks were there. The moves were working. Everything looked perfect. Julius was second on his team in scoring, behind Moses Malone, the 76ers' new go-to guy. And he was landing 51.7 percent of his shots, with a 21.4-point average per game.

In the Eastern Conference Finals, the 76ers romped over the New York Knicks in four games, scoring over 100 points in all but one of them. Then in the finals, the 76ers faced their old enemy, the Los Angeles Lakers. It promised to be a real gun-and-run battle, and it was. But it was all one-sided. The 76ers trounced them in four straight games, with Julius pumping in 7 points during the final minute and a half of the last game.

It was the crowning touch. Dr. J had made it. He'd led his team to an NBA championship!

Bobby Jones, Dr. J's teammate and an exciting player in his own right, said of his friend, "Many superstars have an attitude of 'Nobody is good enough to play with me.' Or 'I'm so much better than the rest of the team that I can be aloof.' Julius was just the opposite of that. He was the kind of guy who built his teammates up."

How? Bobby tells the story: "I remember one particular game when one of the players had two free-throws with three or four seconds to go. We had a chance to win the game if he would have made them. He missed them both. Julius was the first guy into the locker room. He went over beside the guy who missed the shots and said, 'Hey, don't worry about it. We'll get it next time.' He was an encourager. He was the kind of guy you like to have in your foxhole, and I always appreciated that about Julius. He was there for you when you needed him."[7]

That 1983 season was Philadelphia's and Julius's last championship. He would play for four more years and continue to excel. But a basketball player only has so many championship years in him, and in 1987, Julius realized it was time to quit.

But not without a show. In his second-to-last game, at age 37, he scored 38 points, as his mother, wife, and children looked on. And he crossed the 30,000 mark in total points.

In 1992, he was elected to the Basketball Hall of Fame.

Julius Erving's legacy is a reputation and name that many revere and many more admire. Dominique Wilkins summed up his career with these words: "I've never heard anyone knock him or express jealousy. Never one negative word. I can't name you one other player who has that status."[8]

David L. Andrews, a sportswriter, said of him, "Julius Erving was arguably the most complete basketball player of all time. His skill, grace, and commitment dominated the professional game for over fifteen years. However, without his caring, supportive, and unselfish attitude, Julius would not have become the great champion that he was. Julius was not only a great player, he was also a great person."[9]

That's quite a legacy. And something to aspire to for those Christians who seek to imitate the good Doctor, Dr. J, Julius Erving!

---

1. Lincoln Library of Sports Champions, vol. 5 (Columbus, Ohio: Frontier Press, 1992), 82.
2. *Lincoln Library*, 82.
3. *Lincoln Library*, 82.
4. *Lincoln Library*, 78.
5. Dave Branon, *Slam Dunk* (Chicago: Moody, 1994), 75.
6. Branon, 76–77.
7. Branon, 78.
8. Branon, 79.
9. David L. Andrews, *Great Athletes*, vol. 5 (Pasadena, Calif.: Salem Press, 1992), 717.

☆ David Robinson ☆

©Allsport

Chapter 2

Height: 7 feet, 1 inch

Weight: 250 pounds

Position: Center

Birth date: August 6, 1965

Team: **San Antonio Spurs**

David Robinson: Mr. Robinson's Neighborhood

David Robinson could have joined the San Antonio Spurs two years earlier than 1989 if he had done one thing: quit the U.S. Naval Academy before his junior year and transferred to a top-ten basketball school.

But he chose not to.

Why? Because he valued two things: a good education and loyalty.

When he decided to stay at the Naval Academy, he knew that he might never play in the NBA. But he said that wouldn't break his heart. There were important things in life besides basketball.

Of course, no one could have predicted what did happen. After graduating from the Naval Academy with a B-plus average and being named the best college player in the country in 1986–87, David owed five years to the Navy. Five years off the courts and out of practice might have done him in. But others had delayed the pros and survived. Football Hall of Famer Roger Staubach gave his five years and still went on to fame and glory with the Dallas Cowboys.

But then something of a miracle happened for David. Navy Secretary James Webb decided that because David was seven feet tall, he couldn't fit into Navy submarines. He wouldn't be needed for all five years. "Do two," he told David in so many words.

And David Robinson was on his way to bringing San Antonio out of the cellar and making a mark as one of the NBA's best centers.

But before he got to the NBA he'd already done some important basketball business.

David's parents soon realized they had one smart kid on their hands when David was growing up. When his mother took him grocery shopping, she used him to figure out the cost of products by the ounce. At the same time, David added up the bill before they reached the checkout counter. He was always correct—to the penny.

When David was fifteen, his father bought a kit for a six-foot projection TV. The Navy, though, called David's dad for sea duty while he was in the middle of assembling it. When Dad returned three weeks later, David had assembled the whole TV. Dad was a sonar technician, so he was pretty amazed at David's feat. But David had already decided he wanted to be like his number one hero, his dad. He wanted to join the Navy and major in electronics.

David only played basketball one year in high school, his senior year. He was six feet, seven inches tall. And he'd never done anything on the basketball court except play in pickup games. He wasn't that interested. He liked academics better, as well as baseball and gymnastics.

But the high school guidance counselor and basketball coach talked him into coming out. Osbourn Park High School in Manassas, Virginia, needed some new blood. In the first game, the regular center got injured and David played in his place. He scored 14 points with 14 rebounds. He was on his way.

College coaches scouted out Osbourn Park's team and noticed David. By season's end, he was averaging 15 points a game with 12 rebounds. The Navy coach, Paul Evans, also happened by. He liked what he saw. When he learned that David had already applied for admission to the Academy because of its academics, not its rather inferior basketball program, he was pleased.

His freshman year, David mostly rode the wood, but he frequently came off the bench to fill in. He averaged over 7 points a game and 4 rebounds. And he hit 62 percent from the field. Not bad for a bench man. The team went 24–8, the first time in history Navy had won over 20 games in a season. At that point, the coach saw stardom ahead. David was still growing, he learned fast, and he was eager—all good signs for a basketball player.

After that year, the coach had a talk with David. He told him that he could become one of the game's best players. However, he had to want it. And he'd have to work hard—harder than he'd ever worked in his life.

The coach's words struck him. David's second year at Navy, he took the Midshipmen (the name of the team) to a 26–6 season, better than the previous year by two games. He scored 23.6 points a game and dragged down over 11 rebounds. He blocked 128 opposition shots, too. What's more, Navy became the Colonial Conference champion and was invited to the National Collegiate Athletic Association (NCAA) Tournament, which brought in sixty-four of the best teams in the country to do battle for the number one spot.

Navy beat Louisiana State in the first round, but then lost to the University of Maryland, at that time one of the ten best teams in the United States.

David came home unhappy but fulfilled. He had taken his team farther than they'd ever gone before.

But now it was time to make the decision. Should he stay on at the Naval Academy and face five years of service after graduation, or should he transfer to a top-ten school and go right into the NBA after college?

It was a rough choice. But David opted for learning and loyalty, the kind of decision that fit his image as a gentleman and an all-round good person. He wasn't yet a Christian, but the quality of his attitude contributed to leading him to his close and committed walk with the Lord.

Returning to Navy as a junior, David had glory still ahead of him. He led the team to a 35–5 season, the best in Navy's history. He averaged 22.7 points and 13 rebounds per game. And he was named an all-American. He also set new NCAA records for most blocked shots in a game (14), and in a season (207).

That year, the NCAA Tournament was even better. The Middies started off against the Syracuse Orangemen, the team ranked seventh in the country. Their center, a loudmouth named Rony Seikaly, boasted that they would have no problem beating the "shorthairs" from Navy. It was an insult, and David decided to exact revenge on Seikaly. He wanted to hold the center to 4 points.

Sure enough, Syracuse was tromped by the so-called shorthairs. Seikaly didn't score more than 4 points and even had one shot jammed back into his face by Robinson. A Syracuse backup center fouled out trying to stop David, too. Meanwhile, the Aircraft Carrier, as David was being called, romped with 35 points, 11 rebounds, and 7 blocked shots. Score: 97–85. A rout. And an upset.

After Syracuse, Navy polished off Cleveland State. Then it was the powerful Duke University in the third round. Duke's Blue Devils won, but David's wish had been granted. Navy had gone farther in the NCAA than ever, farther than they could ever have dreamed without him.

In the next year's NCAA Tournament, Navy was stopped by Michigan, but only after David scored 50 points in the game. That year, he was third in the country in average points scored per game (28.2), fourth in rebounds (11.8), and first in blocked shots (4.5). He was now owner of three NCAA blocked-shots records that still stand: career, 516; season, 207; and game, 14.

He had also set thirty-three Navy records, including most career points (2,669), most career rebounds (1,314), most career blocked shots (516), most career steals (160), and highest career field-goal percentage (.613). He was voted college basketball's top player, took away all the player-of-the-year awards, and even won the Sullivan Award, which is given to the top amateur athlete in the United States. On the speech stump, he told kids to keep to the books and keep far away from drugs. He signed a multitude of autographs with the words, "Stay in school, David Robinson." More than all this, he was popular and well liked as a person. On and off the court, tough as he was, he remained friendly, talkative, and kind to those who sought him out.

The next two years, David worked in the Navy as a supervisor in the building of submarines. Still, the NBA wasn't going to wait. San Antonio drafted him with the very first pick of the first round. They brought him to the city, wined and dined him, and offered him a $26-million, eight-year contract, the highest ever paid at that point.

San Antonio needed a go-to guy, and they had decided that David was him, even if they had to wait for two years until he was out of the Navy. They were nearly the worst team in the NBA, and they had no ranked center. They were also losing fans. Only 8,000 showed up per game, which was second worst among the twenty-three NBA teams. They needed a winner, so they went after David for all they were worth.

After he visited San Antonio and saw how they welcomed him, David knew he'd found home. He signed.

The next event on the agenda was the 1988 Olympics in Seoul, South Korea. The U.S. basketball team had won the gold medal in nine out of the previous eleven Olympics. In 1988, with people like David on the team, everyone thought they were a shoo-in.

They weren't. They easily defeated six teams, but then they ran hard up against the Soviets. They played poorly, and the Russians played smart. In an upset, the Soviets won, 82–76. The best David could hope for was a bronze medal, which the Americans did capture from Australia in the next game.

David felt deeply disappointed. He had wanted a gold medal as much as any other Olympic athlete, and he felt let down.

But that didn't stop him. In 1989, he joined the Spurs. Their record the previous year was 21–61, one of the worst in the league. The people of San Antonio expected David to double those win stats.

The team was filled out with forward Terry Cummings (who would become one of David's best friends), point guard Maurice "Mo" Cheeks, and Sean Elliott, a six-foot-eight-inch forward.

That first night on the court, November 4, 1989, the Spurs played the previous year's NBA champions, the Los Angeles Lakers. If they did well, many thought, it might be an omen. David threw up shortly before he ran out onto the court. He said it was the Mexican food he'd had earlier in the evening, not the jitters. But who knew?

David quickly tore up the court with 23 points and 17 rebounds. The Spurs whipped the previous year's world champions, 106–98. San Antonio was on air.

Soon, David was being compared to the best centers in basketball—Hakeem Olajuwon of the Houston Rockets and Patrick Ewing of the New York Knicks. Although David was big, he had speed, grace, and agility. He could run like a guard and he possessed a number of moves that made him perfect for blocking shots, something he'd perfected long ago in the Navy. Plus he could shoot, stuff, and play in the lane as well as any other center or forward.

David finished the 1989–90 season with 24.3 points and 12.0 rebounds per game. He was also third-best in the league in blocked shots, with 3.9 per game. Those stats won him sixth place in the vote for NBA MVP (Magic Johnson won it that year).

Things were happening in the stadium, too; San Antonio's attendance nearly doubled, to 14,700 fans per game. The fans liked David's style. He was especially good with kids and participated in various programs to keep youngsters away from drugs.

Meanwhile, the Spurs went 56–26, double their win total from the year before. What was more, they beat the Celtics' similar turnaround with rookie Larry

Bird in 1980 by three games (the Celtics turned around 32 games that year).

That year, the Spurs also went to the playoffs. They knocked off the Denver Nuggets in the first round, 3–0. But then they ran up against the Portland Trail Blazers, who had the number two record in the NBA. It was a tough contest that the teams split the first six games, 3–3. Then in the seventh, David bucked with Kevin Duckworth the whole game. The Spurs made a bad pass, fouled in the last few seconds, and lost the game.

Season over.

But that wasn't the end of it for the Admiral. That year David played in the NBA All-Star Game and was named Rookie of the Year. He also made the NBA All-Defensive Team, the all-NBA third team, and won the Schick Pivotal Player Award. It was one great season, and David had shown his top form. But he would go only higher.

The 1990–91 season saw David performing before sellout crowds the whole year in San Antonio. The team went 55–27, won their division, and moved on to the playoffs with glory on their minds. David led the NBA in rebounds and blocked shots, and was scoring more points than the previous year with an even higher shooting percentage. People were now comparing David to Hall of Famer and defensive player extraordinaire, Bill Russell. But while David had many of the defensive gifts that

Russell had, he was better on offense. Russell's scoring average was never more than 19 points per game while David's average never dipped under 23. And David had a better shooting percentage than Russell—.533 to .440.

But what did the comparisons matter at that point? David was only in his second year. He had another ten or more in the pros before the real comparisons could be made.

It's a special mark of pride to David that he has been named to the NBA All-Defensive Team every year he's been in the league. One reason for that distinction is because he's left-handed. Men playing against him are used to making moves on righties and when they come up against David, their timing is thrown off. Add to that David's portfolio of amazing defensive moves, and you've got the number one shot blocker in the NBA.

It was during the 1990–91 season that David also became a Christian. He had an earlier encounter with faith in 1986 while flying back from the world basketball championships in Spain. On the same flight sat a number of evangelists who had attended a meeting. One of them took a seat next to David and started talking to him about Jesus. After some discussion, he said, "Do you want to pray?" David prayed, but he admitted later he didn't really understand what the evangelist was talking about.

However, the experience stuck with him, and he thought about it as he wondered what life was all about, who had made him, and where he was going. They weren't bothersome questions, they simply nagged at the back of his mind in free moments.

David had grown up in a Christian family and had always attended church as a kid. When he joined the Spurs, a chaplain gave him some Bible study materials, but he didn't pay much attention to them.

Then a minister from Austin, Greg Ball, who represented a group called Champions for Christ, came by to visit David in his home. He asked only a few questions, one of which was, "Do you love God?"

David said, "Yeah, I guess," thinking it would be stupid to say he didn't.

Then Greg asked, "How much time do you spend praying and talking to Him? How much time do you spend reading the Word?"

David said, "I think I have a Bible around here somewhere." He was embarrassed to admit he didn't even know where it was.

Greg countered, "Well, for the people that you love, you really make time for them. You want to get to know them, and you have a heart for them."

For David, it was a moment of revelation. "He showed me I didn't have a heart toward God. He really convicted me that day, and that day I made a commitment to the Lord." He prayed, "Lord, I want to learn everything I can about You. I want to give every-thing to You because You have really blessed me."

From that point on, David Robinson was a changed man.[1]

Later, in 1993, the Admiral, with his Christian friends Avery Johnson and David Wood, sponsored a teen evangelistic rally called "Jammin' Against the Darkness." Over 11,000 men and kids showed up at San Antonio's HemisFair Arena. They listened to the inspired speaking of the three NBA stars, as well as other presenters, and many received Christ. It became the biggest crusade ever in San Antonio's history.

After his conversion, David continued to play bet-ter and better ball, feeling in some sense he was playing for Someone other than just the Spurs and the San Antonio fans. In 1993, averaging 23.4 points per game with a field-goal percentage of .501, he led the Spurs to another winning record and into the playoffs. In 1994, he exceeded those numbers with 29.8 points per game, and a field-goal percentage of .507, third highest in the NBA. He also ranked high in blocked shots with 265, and averaged over 10 rebounds per game. He was edged out by Hakeem Olajuwon for MVP, but claimed a strong and decisive second place.

Whether or not David Robinson will lead the Spurs to an NBA championship is yet to be seen. He ranks among the top four centers in the NBA—Ewing of the Knicks, Olajuwon of the Rockets, and

Shaquille O'Neal of the Magic are all pushing for the number-one spot. Already, though, after only six years in the NBA, David is considered Hall of Fame material.

But what matters most to him is his family and his walk with the Lord. With that kind of attitude, he'll continue to go far—in faith and in life.

---

1.   David Branon, *Slam Dunk* (Chicago: Moody, 1994), 224–225.

Chapter 3

Height: 6 feet

Weight: 175 pounds

Position: Guard

Birth date: June 1, 1969

Team: **Charlotte Hornets**

☆ Tony Bennett ☆

©Allsport

Tony Bennett: Mr. Basketball

Tony Bennett earned his nickname, Mr. Basketball, during his senior year at Preble High School in his home town of Green Bay, Wisconsin. Although he played serious basketball in junior high, he had not set his sights on the NBA; he simply wanted to play well. He knew, though, that if he did play well, the NBA might someday take interest in him and leave a calling card.

He was not wrong about that!

In high school he worked hard, dribbling and shooting against his sister Kathy, who also played in high school. She is six years older than Tony, and for a long time could best him. But by the time Tony had completed high school, she had stopped playing against him. He was just too good, too basketball, too "Mr. Basketball."

His teammates at Preble were small; most of the guys were under six feet, as was Tony, who didn't reach six feet until college. Tony says now, "We weren't a real strong team, but we had great chemistry, and we were just a bunch of short guys who could shoot the lights out. It was a blast. People never expected anything from us. People would look at us and start laughing in warm-ups, but we could play."[1]

At the time, Tony's dad, Dick, was head basketball coach at the University of Wisconsin, Green Bay. Tony met a young player there named Terry Porter, now a famed point guard for the Portland Trail Blazers. He and Terry spent a lot of time going one-on-one during practice and eventually became good friends. Terry became a kind of older brother for Tony. Tony says, "Every year I had the opportunity to be around the gym and my father. When I was a sophomore, I got to play with the college guys at Green Bay. That was a benefit for me, going up against guys who were so much more physically mature."[2]

That experience helped prepare Tony for the days ahead. After his excellent seasons at Preble

High several colleges were recruiting him. But there was no contest. He wanted to play for his dad at UW-Green Bay. Like Pete Maravich, who in the 1970s played for his own father at LSU, Tony had several reasons he wanted to play for his dad. One, his father knew Tony's style of play and how it fit into a team situation better than any other coach. Two, Coach Bennett knew how to get the most out of his players; he knew how to stretch them. Tony believed that if he wanted to play in the NBA, he needed that kind of training and experience.

Any father-son relationship in college or professional sports is tough. Pete Maravich and his father, Press, were well known for both their problems and their successes. Pete hadn't even wanted to go to LSU to play for his father because LSU ranked as a second-level basketball school. But his father almost forced Pete into it.

There was none of that kind of strife in Tony's relationship with his father. Quite apart from any family relationship, Tony idolized his dad and considered him an excellent coach. He'd worked his way up in the UW structure, coaching teams in London (Wisconsin), Eau Claire, and Stevens Point before arriving at Green Bay. His success guaranteed him an up and running position in college basketball.

What's more, Tony's father longed to develop his son's talent, and in light of Tony's NBA ambitions, he wanted to be part of getting his son there.

Tony's years at UW-Green Bay were stellar. He set several NCAA records, including shooting 49.7 percent from the three-point line (290 baskets for 584 attempts). He was leading scorer in the Mid-Continent Conference (1991–92), of which UW-Green Bay was a part, and logged 2,285 points and 601 assists during his career. He holds twenty-two offensive records at UW-Green Bay, too, including scoring leader, most assists, and highest free throw percentage in a single game. He ended up Mid-Continent Conference Player of the Year in 1992, and in the postseason tournament he was MVP.

No dummy, Tony also maintained a grade point average of 3.46. As a result he was named to the GTE Academic All-America Team.

Tony's spiritual life by that time had solidified. He grew up in a strongly Christian home where he learned about morals and good values and belief in God from his parents. During his ninth-grade year he began thinking about heaven, death, and the afterlife. He knew he wanted to go to heaven when he died, but he wasn't quite sure how to get there.

That year he went to a Christian sports camp, where he heard the gospel. After listening to several presentations, Tony realized the message made sense. He was ripe. So he committed himself to the

Lord and began a walk that continues to this day. He credits his decision for Christ as the most important one in his life, even beyond that of going to UW-Green Bay to play for his father, and that of playing for the Charlotte Hornets.

One of the highlights of playing for UW-Green Bay was the final season game of Tony's junior year. It was against Northern Illinois. ESPN broadcast the game live. After UW-Green Bay won the game, the players and crowd went into instant pandemonium. Tony was mobbed on the court but he made his way out, looking for his dad. His father hadn't escaped the celebration ritual. Players dumped Gatorade all over him and he was soaking wet. But he was looking for his son.

They met at mid-court. The crowd broke. And Tony and his father embraced in a long, joyous victory hug there in front of all the cameras. Tony says it was "an awesome feeling."

Long before, Dick Bennett had told Tony, "Good basketball knows no divisions or limits. It doesn't matter where you're from, what school you go to, what reputation you have, when you're out on the court, if you can play, you can play, and nothing can take that away."[3]

That advice would stick with Tony through all those years of moving up the ladder toward the NBA. In 1991, he had an opportunity to play in the Pan American Games with teammates like Christian

Laettner, Jimmy Jackson, and Walt Williams. Tony was the starting point guard. He remained confident, unawed as he went up against the best players in North and South America. Once again, his father's advice proved right on target. Tony could play, and all could see it.

By the end of the 1992 college season, Tony had racked up 2,285 career points, hitting an average of 19.4 per game, with a field-goal percentage of 52.8. In 1991–92 alone he hit 95 for 196 three-pointers, striking fire 48 percent of the time.

These impressive stats, though, would not make getting to the NBA easy. Plenty of excellent players end up in the CBA (Continental Basketball Association) just hoping for a ten-day contract into the NBA to strut and shoot their stuff. Tony knew it would take some work despite his record at UW-Green Bay. So he participated in a predraft camp in Chicago where scouts would be watching in order to make recommendations to their teams for the draft. Tony also attended the NBA camp in Orlando that same year.

This was serious business. Here were men competing for millions of dollars in salaries and benefits. Here were the general managers and coaches of the most well known basketball teams in the world. And here were men struggling with every inch of their being to be noticed. Tony felt the strain and found himself asking hard questions about his priorities. What really mattered to him now? Did he want this?

Yes. He says, "It made me realize that all these things we are doing are temporary. Important, but temporary. You've got to enjoy it and go after it, but there is something more important. And that's the thing that lasts and that's permanent. And that's my faith in Christ. It's the relationship I have with my family."[4]

The confidence that grows out of such faith helped Tony relax and make all the minute adjustments necessary to get noticed. The Charlotte Hornets liked what they saw and they drafted Tony in the second round, thirty-fifth overall pick. Charlotte had taken Alonzo Mourning with their first pick.

It was a high moment. Tony would be playing with new and notorious players like Larry Johnson, Muggsy Bogues, and Del Curry. There were other old-timers like Hersey Hawkins and Kenny Gattison to round out the roster. Keeping up with those guys would be tough.

His rookie season brought with it the usual hazing and mocking that all new players go through. Before one game, the players told Tony that his job as rookie was to lead the charge out onto the court at the start of the game. Tony was ready. He rampaged at full sprint out onto the court as the lights came up. Then he turned around and found himself all alone at center court. His teammates stood back in the tunnel laughing hysterically.

Tony laughs off most of the gags. If not for his love of the Lord, though, he might be singing another tune. He believes his commitment to Christ is essential to his success. He told one reporter, "Every day I wake up, I'm thankful for my health and this opportunity. I'm doing the Lord's work. I'm a Christian basketball player who has a love for the Lord."[5]

He keeps a Bible verse in the back of his mind at all times. Proverbs 27:21: "The crucible for silver and the furnace for gold, but man is tested by the praise he receives."

He knows the meaning of that verse. Every time he plays he feels the impact of praise, evaluation, criticism, and being a role model. He knows the pressure and tries to live above it in the power of the Spirit.

The highlight of his rookie season, he says, was stuffing the Boston Celtics in the playoffs. The Boston Celtics—granddaddy of all teams in the NBA. The Hornets bumped them out of the playoffs in the first round, 3–1. In the next round, New York made mincemeat out of the young Hornets, 4–1. But it was all in good competition.

In the 1992–93 season, Tony played in 75 games and threw in 276 points for an average of 3.7. Not bad for a playmaker and point guard. In 1993–94, he had similar stats: 74 games, 248 points, 3.4 average.

Tony takes his success with a level head. In the many high school and camp appearances that he makes, Tony tells kids, "All the stuff I've experienced is great and I'm very blessed because I know the Lord has given me great opportunities. Being in the limelight, having my face on basketball cards, driving a nice car, making money, and playing in front of all these people is great, but I say: 'It's going to go away someday. It is going to go away. It's not lasting. You also have to put your time and your effort into the thing that is permanent.' For me, that is my faith in Jesus Christ and my relationship to Him and my family and friends."[6]

Good words for anyone who aspires to the place Tony occupies today.

---

1. David Branon, Slam Dunk (Chicago: Moody, 1994), 22.
2. Branon, 23.
3. Branon, 21–22.
4. Branon, 27.
5. Rick Hines and Rob Bentz, "A Good First Impression," *Sports Spectrum*, November 1993, 7.
6. Branon, 28–29.

☆ Kevin Johnson ☆

Height: 6 feet, 1 inch
Weight: 190 pounds
Position: Guard
Birth date: March 4, 1966
Team: **Phoenix Suns**

Chapter 4

Kevin Johnson: At the Point

Kevin Johnson once thought he might play pro baseball. After all, he had been all-city in high school.

So, in his third year of college, he traveled to Modesto, California, to play on one of the Oakland Athletics' minor league teams. He played shortstop in two games, batted twice, scored a run, and made one error. That was it.

The coach slashed him off the roster. Cut!

End of baseball career.

Kevin knew he had to get rolling on his other favorite sport if he wanted to make any kind of mark. So he hunkered down on basketball.

Not that he hadn't been working at it a long time. Kevin played well in high school. He led his league in scoring, 32.5 points per game, with 56 points scored in one game. Colleges came scouting and offering scholarships. And suddenly, Kevin was bound from Sacramento to Berkeley to play for the University of California.

It was during those years that Kevin discovered a genuine commitment to Jesus. It had started in high school. One day Kevin got bored in geometry class and asked a B-ball team friend, "What's this thing about Jesus?" The friend invited Kevin to church. Kevins's family—his mother and grandparents—were not churchgoers and he hadn't been in church since he was five or six years old. But Kevin was interested and went with his friend. When he heard the gospel, he knew what he wanted. He accepted Christ.

That was only the beginning. He wandered along the paths of faith for the next few years and stayed mostly off the track. He knew he needed to be more focused, but he couldn't seem to find the right groove.

Then in his junior year at UC, he realized he didn't really know what it meant to be a Christian. He picked up a New Testament and decided to read a chapter a night until he'd gotten all the way through. By the time he finished, he knew he was a Christian for real. He considers that time his real conversion.

Kevin's faith didn't exactly make an big impact on his college performance. He was scoring an average of 14 points a game, not especially impressive, even though he did make all-Pacific 10, a  league honor. He set some school records as well: points scored (1,655), assists (423), and steals (155). He also came up with something called a "triple-double." A "double-double" happens when a player reaches double digits in points and rebounds in a game. A triple-double occurs when he hits double digits in three categories: scoring, rebounds, and assists. In one game Kevin logged 22 points, tore down 10 rebounds, and dished out 12 assists. Pretty good for a point guard and playmaker who's supposed to get the ball to the go-to guy.

It was more than enough to make the pros sit up and scout—and finally recommend drafting Kevin. Kevin was drafted in the first round, seventh pick overall. He was headed for Cleveland and Cavalierland.

Kevin's mom often asked him, "Kevin, do you want to be special?" She meant that to be successful you had to be different. In the Sacramento ghetto neighborhood Kevin grew up in, that meant watching out for yourself, keeping your nose clean, and your toes out of all dirty business. Gangs inhabited every corner of the streets. Druggies roamed freely and pushers pushed their drugs. It was a dangerous time and a dangerous place to be.

Kevin decided to follow his mother's advice. He wanted to be "special"—different. But he decided to take it a step further. He would learn not just how to survive; no, he would learn how to succeed.

When the Cavaliers called on K. J. to take the point, they didn't realize they already had another sparkler at that position: Mark Price, another Christian and a close friend of Kevin's. After Kevin spent half a year with the Cavs, the management decided they didn't need two stellar point guards. They decided to deal with the Phoenix Suns. Eventually a trade was agreed on for Kevin, two other players, and several first and second draft picks. The Cavs got Larry Nance and Mike Sanders.

That was fine by Kevin. He had loved the weather in California, but living in Cleveland, Ohio, where the sun rarely shone, was difficult. Phoenix would be a return to a warm, sunny climate.

Kevin immediately found a close fit with his new team. The Suns were building for ultimate NBA stardom, and players like Charles Barkley could excel even more with Kevin's quickness, passing ability, and playmaking finesse. Tom Felton writes of

Kevin's contribution to the Suns in *Sports Spectrum:* "If you want flat out foot speed, you've come to the right person. K.J. has long been regarded as one of the fastest players in the game. His speed and quickness have enabled him to penetrate defenses for easy lay-ups and pinpoint passes. In the 1990–91 NBA season he became only the fifth player in the history of the game to average more than 20 points and 10 assists."[1]

With those kinds of stats, Kevin is well on his way. He is considered one of the best point guards in the NBA, ranked alongside his old teammate, Mark Price. In his first seven seasons with the Suns, Kevin has thrown through 9,424 points, with an 18.6-point average. In 1989–90, he had his best scoring year, with 22.5 points per game. He has shot 49.4 percent from the field during his career, and has doled out 4,912 assists. For three years in a row (1989–91) he was named to the all-NBA second team, and he has played in three all-star games.

The highlight, though, of his career was the Suns' 1993 attempt to unseat the Chicago Bulls and Michael Jordan from the NBA championship. That series goes down in history as one of the toughest-fought battles ever. That year, the Suns went into the finals with their best season record ever, 62–20. Even the Bulls hadn't played that well (they were 57–25). But no matter where the Bulls were in the standings, there was one person everyone had to take into account: Michael Jordan. Anything was possible with him in the contest.

The first two games in Phoenix were disasters for K. J. He scored only 15 points and assisted 8 times in two games. He was low.

But Coach Paul Westphal, also a Christian, decided to make some changes. In the first two games, K. J. had been covering the Bulls' play-maker, B. J. Armstrong. At one point their matchup even led to a scuffle. It was clearly a mismatch as far as the coach was concerned. As Kevin lay in bed watching television, Westphal announced he was making some changes. Kevin would cover Michael Jordan the next night. Kevin just pulled the sheets over his head and went to sleep.

The next morning, Kevin read the book of Job for his devotions. He says, "Job had to go through a lot, but at least God didn't visit the plague called Michael Jordan upon him."[2]

Still, he was sure nothing could be worse than that second game. The Phoenix crowd had actually booed Kevin as he came off the floor at Westphal's request late in the game. "Sir Charles" Barkley was incensed. He said, "If you're going to boo Kevin Johnson or give him a hard time when he's strug-gling, please don't come to the game. We've come too far to put up with that [stuff]."[3]

Kevin read Barkley's words in the papers and was encouraged. He had his team behind him even if he hadn't played well.

Now, on to Michael Jordan.

Game three was played in Chicago, and it was one boisterous game. Kevin played like a madman—or should we say, like "someone special." He "held" Michael Jordan to 44 points, which was low for His Airness. During the fourth quarter plus three overtimes Jordan made only 6 of his 20 attempts. Kevin was hot.

K. J. himself scored 25 points, had 9 assists, and collected 7 rebounds. And because the game went for three five-minute overtime periods, in addition to the standard 48 minutes, he played 62 bone-wearying minutes, an NBA finals record. The Suns won, 129–121. It wasn't the highest scoring game in history, but it was a scorcher for stellar performances.

The Suns lost the next game, but they came back and won their last game in Chicago, 108–98. That brought the team back to home turf in Phoenix. Kevin was raring for a contest. The series stood at 3–2. Phoenix had to win to stay alive.

And it was a close contest. In the last few seconds, the Bulls had the ball, two points behind, 98–96. Then John Paxson received a pass out at the three-point line. He threw the ball up. And through. Three points.

Game over. Series over. The Bulls had just three-peated—NBA champion three times in a row. Michael Jordan would retire that year, and NBA basketball would somehow be changed forever.

But not Kevin Johnson. He walks with his Lord, plays his defense, runs his plays, and still sends down 18 to 20 points a game.

And K. J. hasn't forgotten his roots in Sacramento, either. There, he has established St. Hope Academy, a community center for kids. About seventy-five kids each year participate in programs where they learn the principles of success and growth. They memorize Scripture, read the Bible, learn about Jesus, and sometimes see their role model, Kevin, when he's in town.

As a result of his neighborhood-building efforts, Kevin has received numerous awards, including being named a "point of light" by President George Bush.

If Kevin hadn't become a basketball or baseball player, he says today, he'd like to have been a teacher. He's always had a rapport with kids.

Maybe he'd make a good preacher too. What does he tell the kids who come to St. Hope Academy?

"I think there are seven things you have to do on a regular basis to keep your relationship with Christ strong. You have to pray on a regular basis," he says. "Second, you try to read. I think that the more I can read and understand different people's perspectives on Christianity . . . the stronger I'm going to be."

Kevin also advises young people "to take the Bible and study it. You have to try to study what Christ and his disciples were trying to tell the people. You have to take those messages and make them applicable in your everyday life. You have to memorize Scripture and meditate on the Word. You have to hear the Word, and you have to go to church."[4]

That's good advice coming from anyone, but especially someone as "special" as Kevin Johnson.

---

1. Tom Felton, "Something Special," Sports Spectrum, February 1994, 18.
2. Phil Taylor, "A Happy Turn to a Horror Story," *Sports Illustrated*, June 21, 1993, 22.
3. Taylor, 22–23.
4. David Branon, *Slam Dunk* (Chicago: Moody, 1994), 144.

☆ **Mark Jackson** ☆

Height: 6 feet, 3 inches

Weight: 192 pounds

Position: Guard

Birth date: April 1, 1965

Team: **Indiana Pacers**

Chapter 5

Mark Jackson: Making a Mark

The awesome New York Knicks chose him as their number one draft pick in 1987, the eighteenth pick overall. He had been a star at St. John's, setting records in scoring and assists. He had proven himself a powerful point guard who could lead an offense. And he has shown his dribble, fake, and pass in numerous playoff games.

But he's never been on a team that won a title. Maybe he is now.

The Indiana Pacers almost made it into the NBA finals, but they lost the Eastern Conference Finals to New York in 1994. They played tough. And so did Mark Jackson.

Mark Jackson keeps his hopes up.

Mark grew up in New York, and in his first year with the Knicks, he even lived at home with his parents. He didn't need to. He wanted to. He didn't even have his own room. He bunked with his brothers.

Some way to start out his rookie year!

But he didn't mind it at all. He says, "When I was a rookie, I stayed at home with my parents and my family. That was a great time. You know, here I am— 20,000 people screaming and going crazy every time I step on the floor, and the city going crazy— and I'm coming home and just being a regular guy. I still have to clean up and pick up after myself, and I didn't even have my own room. I was sharing it with my brothers.

"It kept me down to earth, but more than that, it showed me the important things in life. Sharing and caring and being around family members. The gift of both parents alive and healthy, brothers and sisters— that's precious and that's something I didn't want to let go, and I never want to let go."[1]

That commitment to family and friends has always marked Mark Jackson. It's part of what led him to the Lord a few years after he joined the pros. It happened during his third year as a Knick. He met a young woman named Desiree and asked her out. On their first date, she shared her faith in Christ with Mark, making it clear that this was the most important thing in her life. No one had ever told Mark about Jesus before that, even though he had gone to Catholic schools and to a Catholic university. Mark thought, "This lady is really special. She just saved my life."

He became a Christian that night, later married that lady, and has never looked back. His faith is an important element of his life, both on and off the court. He tries to share that faith everywhere he goes, whether it's speaking to kids in high school gyms, or at colleges, or in the chapels the teams hold before games.

What does he want more than anything else?

"Perfection," he says. "Wanting to be the best. Wanting to prove people wrong. And most important, wanting to touch lives. Wanting people who sit in the stands or sit watching the TV to say, 'There's something about that guy. Not his basketball ability, not that he can pass the ball and make people around him better, but there's a special light shining in him.' And wanting them to want the same thing and letting them know that the light is Jesus Christ."[2]

How has Mark's career gone?

It started off like rockets. That first year with the Knicks was golden and a real career highlight. He was named Rookie of the Year and played on the all-star team. He says, "Sitting in the locker room with Michael Jordan and Magic Johnson and Larry Bird and those guys. And I'm sitting there, a kid from New York City, who had a dream. I'm sitting in the locker room with these guys, putting on an all-star jersey. That was a phenomenal moment for me."[3]

That year was a marvel all around for Mark. He played in all 82 games, got into the first round of the playoffs, scored 1,114 points for a 13.8 average per game, and had 868 assists, the most ever for a single season for a rookie. He had a high game of 33 points, too.

It was a year of high stats and high spirits. Although New York lost to Boston in the first round of the playoffs, the game still represented a proud moment for Mark. He'd made it to the NBA and he was performing well.

The next year was even better, statistically speaking. He had 619 assists and 1,219 points for a 16.9-point-per-game average. This time New York defeated Boston in the first round of the playoffs, and lost to Chicago in the Eastern Conference Semifinals. Again Mark was ranked for assists, with an 8.6 average.

The next three years for Mark saw a downswing in stats. In 1989–90, he scored only 809 points, a

9.9-point average, with 604 assists. The next year he dropped even lower, scoring only 630 points, an 8.8 average. Some commentators were saying Mark already had his heyday, that he had burned out early and would not long remain in the NBA.

Some media personalities assumed it was those kinds of stats that influenced Mark to come to Christ. But actually, he became a Christian while he was riding high on his first- and second-year successes. Not everyone comes to Jesus when they're hurting or down. It was definitely the influence of a godly woman, Desiree, who spoke to Mark's heart.

But those three off years were not easy. His fifth year with the Knicks saw an updraft to 916 points with a 11.3 average. But a new coach had come aboard with the Knicks and he and Mark had words and conflict. Mark saw no court time in the playoffs. He was literally driven out. A lot of people were saying his attitude was wrong, but in actuality, it was probably more the coach's fault than Mark's.

And it was an important and productive time for Mark, despite the trials. He says, "The thing that I'm very proud about is that I touched more lives through trials and tribulations—not getting any time in the playoffs, not getting any time during the course of the season—I touched more lives during that time than I did being Rookie of the Year and being an all-star, because, simply, I think a man is measured when his back is against the wall. How do you react?

I responded by signing autographs, by going to the malls, still being the same person I've always been. And people were amazed by how positive I was, even though I was going through a struggle. But the main thing is, my trust wasn't in man, my trust was in God, and I thank God for those times."[4]

Mark was traded to the L.A. Clippers in 1992 and saw his figures start back up, averaging 14.4 points per game his first year, and 10.9 his second. And he was coming back as a playmaker, with 678 assists. In fact, he ranked seventh in the NBA in assists.

Then came the Pacers. In Indiana he now plays with Rik Smits, Dale Davis, and Derrick McKey, and he's doing well. He's happy, he's married, and has two children. Nothing gives him more joy than those kids.

And he's looking for an NBA title for his team.

Maybe next year.

---

1. Nancy VanArendonk, "Making His Mark in Indy," *Sports Spectrum*, February 1995, 19.
2. VanArendonk, 19.
3. VanArendonk, 16.
4. VanArendonk, 16.

☆ **Wayman Tisdale** ☆

Height: 6 feet, 9 inches

Weight: 260 pounds

Position: Forward

Birth date: June 9, 1964

Team: **Phoenix Suns**

Wayman Tisdale: Pouring Them In

There was no contest when Wayman Tisdale sifted through his many scholarship offers. It had to be his home state team in the Big Eight Conference, the Oklahoma Sooners. But he didn't know when he started that he would go down in history.

Wayman's years at OU were some of the best of his life. His freshman year he played power forward and poured in 24.5 points per game. He also tugged down 10.3 rebounds. He was selected as an NCAA consensus first-team all-American, the first freshman ever so honored.

The next year only got better. He cranked up his point average to 27.0 per game, and pulled down 9.7 rebounds. Again he made first team NCAA all-American, and this time it was unanimous. That same year, Wayman scorched the nets with an awesome 61 points against the University of Texas at San Antonio. His scoring performance for that game was the national high that year.

During his third year in college, Wayman remained equal to his reputation. He threw in 25.2 points a game and hauled down 10.2 rebounds, setting Oklahoma's all-time point record (2,661) and rebounding record (1,048). The same year he fired 57.8 percent from the field and was again named a unanimous NCAA first-team all-American. He led OU to a top-ten ranking nationally both in 1984 and 1985, their first two ever. Wayman played in the NCAA tournament all of his first three years at OU, leading the Sooners to a 4–3 record in seven games. In the tournament he averaged 22.6 points a game with 9.6 rebounds.

By his second year in college, it was obvious that Wayman would be picked to play for the United States in the Olympics. That year, 1984, he and his teammates took the United States to a gold medal, one of nine won by the United States in thirteen Olympics. He was the leading rebounder on the team, with 6.4 rebounds per game.

The Olympics was, of course, a high point in Wayman's basketball career, but perhaps the biggest moment occurred when the pros came calling. His third year at OU, he decided to make himself available for the NBA draft and not finish college on the regular schedule. The Indiana Pacers, then one of the worst teams in the NBA, drafted him as their first pick in the first round. He was the second pick overall.

Wayman was flying high. Everything was in place. The Pacers were poised to begin some hard-nosed play behind the leadership of their new power forward, and they believed with players like Wayman they would soon be headed for the top of the NBA.

That first year, Wayman played in all but one of the team's 82 games. He averaged 14.7 points and 7.2 rebounds a game. The Pacers, though, didn't do well. They went 26–56, the worst record in the Central Division and the second worst in the NBA. It was a time of disappointment for Wayman, and he turned to his faith in Christ for support and a sense of peace. He says, "Had I not had Christ, it would have worn on me even more. I don't think I would still be playing."[1]

Wayman didn't know then that he was in for a long siege. Although he logged some respectable stats, he would play on losing teams for the next eight years. From 1985 to 1988 he played for the Pacers and dropped in 14.5 points per game in 1986–87, 16.1 in 1987–88, and 17.5 in 1988–89, the year the Pacers traded him in midseason to the Sacramento Kings. His rebounding increased, too. But the losing seasons only continued. Wayman Tisdale was an exile in the NBA—an exile from a winning team.

Here was a million-dollar player who had little to look forward to each season, first with the cellar Pacers and then with the Kings, even though with the Kings, his numbers only increased. He had his best season in 1989—90, with an average of 22.3 points and 7.5 rebounds. His average remained between 16 and 20 points a game for the next four seasons.

Meanwhile, the Kings were piling up losing seasons like ashes in a fireplace. Six seasons burned to smithereens. Nothing to remember, nothing to praise anyone for. Wayman was deeply discouraged and even fearful that his career in the NBA would be marked by nothing but loss.

He prayed and studied his Bible with new fervor. And he poured himself into a second career: jazz music. Recently, he cut an album called *Power Forward*, on which he plays bass guitar and sings his father's favorite song, "Amazing Grace." It's just one of many dreams that are coming true for him off the court. He and David Robinson of the Spurs both possess powerful musical instincts. While David plays piano and sax, Wayman plays bass and sings. Maybe they should get together! Wayman says of his new album, "It's not a Christian album, but I do have some Christian songs on it. People can tell. You get the message."

Music wasn't the only thing looking up, though, this past year. Somehow a miracle happened. Sacramento needed to do some heavy financial reconstruction. Their $2.5-million power forward cost too much, and they decided to let him go.

At first the Los Angeles Clippers talked about a deal that involved several million dollars a year. But Wayman didn't just want money; he wanted to play with a winner.

That was when the Phoenix Suns decided to make an offer. They came across with a deal that was $2 million less than what the Clippers put up.

Read that again: *$2 million less.*

And with the Suns, Wayman wouldn't be the go-to guy, or even necessarily one of the stars. The Suns had six men who had been all-stars, including Charles Barkley, Kevin Johnson, and A. C. Green.

But the Suns had two things that appealed to Wayman: a winning record that could only continue; and three Christians in the front ranks—Johnson, Green, and the coach, Paul Westphal.

Wayman took a $2-million pay cut to play with a winner. And he hasn't looked back.

Weldon Tisdale, Wayman's brother and agent, says, "When [the Suns] called with high interest, we were really impressed—great management and great ownership. Money was not the major issue. Money took a back seat."

In fact, Weldon says, "Wayman was really tired of the losing seasons that he had been through year in and year out. He wanted to get somewhere and win."[2]

Wayman said, "Winning was paramount."

So he took a pay cut and a back seat to some players, and went to Phoenix. In the process, he had to adjust gears numerous times in order to run with a team that already had its many stars and superstars. But Wayman's faith in Christ had solidified years ago when he played on losing NBA teams. Playing with Phoenix, a winning team, was enough to make him feel God was blessing. So now he plays with a huge smile printed on his lips.

He says, "I think that when people see me play they can tell I have Christ in my life. I'm smiling and having a good time. It's because Christ is working through me."[3]

Playing for Phoenix, Wayman dipped from a 17.0 average per game to 10.0. He didn't always start. And he frequently took a back seat to Sir Charles and others.

But all that is eclipsed by the fact that Phoenix was in the playoffs and had a winning record, something Wayman had never been part of in the NBA.

With his music and his basketball, Wayman feels that he has two talents to share with people. He says, "I feel very blessed that the Lord gave me two talents that can reach millions of people. I can reach a certain amount of people through basketball, and musically, even that many more. I want to use those [talents] to the best of my ability, to glorify God. On the court I want people to say, 'Hey, there's something different about him. No matter what the situation was, he always seemed to shine. There's a player who loves the Lord.'"[4]

One of Wayman's highlight games happened on April 12 against the San Antonio Spurs, the leading team in the Western Conference. The Suns were two and a half games out of first place at the time.

Wayman poured it on from the bench, shelling the hoop with a strong showing of 16 points. With 24 seconds left, he sent in a follow-up shot to put the Suns ahead. They won, 115–111.

It was a tremendous triumph for Wayman, and it was the Suns' fifty-fifth win of the year. Wayman had never even seen a 30-win season with the Kings, but now he was rolling on a winning tide that couldn't be stopped.

With his Christian brothers, Kevin Johnson, A. C. Green, and Paul Westphal, Wayman has discovered a powerful sense of fellowship. "It's very rough on the road," he says. "It's really helped me to have such believers and good strong reinforcement. We pray together, and we challenge each other to find out what's been going on in our lives. They've just been a true blessing."[5]

Ultimately, it's his relationship with his family—his wife, Regina and their four children, Danielle, Tiffany, Gabrielle, and Wayman Jr.—and with his Lord that is Wayman's greatest strength. He continues to grow and learn, but most of all to win. And that's a great blessing, too.

"The only way that I'm here today is keeping Christ first in my life and letting him guide my footsteps, because you're not seeing something Wayman Tisdale did; it's something Christ has done for him. He's taught me how to be humble in all of it."[6]

What's the greatest thing that has happened since he became part of a winning team? Wayman says, "It's been great. I mean it's been truly great! I went from being a mediocre, lukewarm Christian to a person who's really on fire."[7]

Well, keep on burning bright, Wayman Tisdale!

---

1. Rob Bentz, "A Place in the Sun," *Sports Spectrum*, June 1995, 18.
2. Bentz, 18.
3. Bentz, 18.
4. Bentz, 19.
5. Bentz, 19.
6. Bentz, 19.
7. Bentz, 19.

☆ Brent Price ☆

Height: 6 feet, 1 inch

Weight: 185 pounds

Position: Guard

Birth date: December 9, 1968

Team: **Washington Bullets**

Brent Price: Points from the Point Guard

What do the following people have in common?

Horace and Harvey Grant

Dick and Tom Van Arsdale

Gerald and Dominique Wilkins

Albert and Bernard King

Mark and Brent Price

Answer: They're all brothers. They all play or played in the NBA. And they all scored against each other at times while their parents cheered them on.

Family rivalries in sports probably go all the way back to the Greeks when Apollos and Paulos battled it out for an Olympic gold medal. In such rivalries, comparisons are frequently made by outsiders. "He's better at laying it up, but his brother can shoot that three-pointer like no one on the court."

Comparisons are probably the worst hazard a sibling faces when playing against a brother on the other roster. But to Brent Price his brother remains a friend, mentor, and hero of sorts. Mark is five years and six NBA seasons older than Brent. Mark has notched up some remarkable stats with the Cleveland Cavaliers; he's an all-star. Brent considers his brother's accomplishments something to aspire to. Brent has played with the Washington Bullets his first three seasons. They haven't been winning seasons, but they have been a time of training and proving himself.

"It's a lot to live up to," Brent says. "Mark has been so many things. It's strange—that's the word, strange—to play against him. Mom and Dad are up there in the stands too. But since Mark is so established in the league right now, they really pull for me while I'm in the game."

Brent has had some good games with the Bullets, but injuries have been a problem. "My first year I was out of the preseason with an injury. And then

74

last year, I had a knee operation and was out for the whole season. I sat on the bench watching the guys play. It was my third year in the NBA and I had hoped to really show what I could do. Now I feel I have to do it all over again."

Brent writes such disappointments off with a strong faith in Christ. "When I was nine years old, I told my parents I wanted to accept Jesus. I'd thought a lot about it in church. We grew up in the church, and my parents were a godly example. So it just seemed natural. Mom, Dad, and I knelt down by my bed and prayed. That was it. But ever since then I've never doubted that God was in my life, leading, helping, building my faith."

It's a powerful testimony that Brent gives whenever he has a chance in the media. The Bullets' chapels, led by their chaplain, Joel Freeman, are a real boost to Brent's faith. He and Joel are good friends. They share a joy in Christ that Brent first developed as a child.

Brent comes from a long line of basketball players. His mother, Ann Price, played under the old six-on-six rules for women and was quite intense on the court. Brent's father, Denny, has coached basketball at several colleges and even worked with the Phoenix Suns from 1974 to 1976. He played semipro, too, and in high school once dumped in 42 points in a championship game. Brent's father still works with him perfecting his outside, three-point, and corner shots.

Brent's parents nurtured all their boys in the faith, basketball, and, strangely enough, music. Brent's mom is an excellent pianist, and his father, with the three brothers, Mark, Matt, and Brent, sang in church and across the state. They witnessed as a family and often led whole crowds of people in song and worship.

Thus, Brent grew up in a home that knew the limelight.

After several excellent years playing high-school basketball, Brent was scouted by George Felton, head coach for the University of South Carolina. He wanted Brent to come there and offered him a scholarship. Brent agreed. It was a good opportunity, even though USC didn't have a high ranking among basketball schools.

At USC, Brent played in 59 games, scored 743 points, and had 206 assists. They were worthy stats, but Brent realized he wanted something bigger, a larger platform on which to show his talent. He knew he wouldn't get attention from the pros if he stayed on in a small school. He needed to get into a college where scouts and coaches would notice him.

So after two years at USC, Brent transferred to the University of Oklahoma, a school ranked in the top ten and a place where Brent, if he played well, might see the pros come calling.

At the time, UO had a very talented team. Just a few years earlier, Wayman Tisdale had made his mark as a power forward. Though Brent was a guard, a tradition of great players like that was hard to ignore. When a scholarship was offered, Brent took off.

He had to sit out the next year because of NCAA rules for transfer students. But he practiced with the team and built a strong rep as an excellent point guard with a sharp three-point shot.

His junior year, he played in 35 games and scored 613 points with 192 assists. But one game stood out from all the others.

It was against Loyola-Marymount on December 15, 1990, and was televised on ESPN. What a circus. Billy Tubbs, the Sooners' coach, informed everyone it would be a high scoring game. Loyola had a reputation for a fast-break, run-and-gun offense. That year, they were second in the nation in average game score with 103 points per game. Oklahoma was right behind them with 96. It looked to be a rousing contest.

Brent says, "We knew from the start it would be a track race. Billy Tubbs as our coach had a goal of being the first coach to score 100 points in a half and 200 points in a game. This looked like the kind of contest that could do that. And when you read the score, you'll see."

Coach Tubbs told Brent that when Loyola took a shot, he wasn't even to wait around for a rebound. He was to take off down the court and look for the ball in the air while he was on the run. Boot and shoot. Run and gun. Whatever you want to call it. "It was one fast break after another, and by the half I was dead," Brent says. "I remember coming off the court breathing hard. But I was really in the zone that night. Everything I threw into the air came down through the hoop."

By the half, the Sooners were creaming Loyola. It was going to be a high score. But in that second half, Brent began throwing up three-point attempts. He was hitting them too, one after another.

Dribble. Shoot. Bing. Three points.

Dribble. Shoot. Bing! More points!

Brent was hotter than he'd ever been. "We call it being in the zone. That's what I was. I was right in the zone. I couldn't miss. Of course I missed some. But everything was going right. Today, whenever I talk to reporters or people who follow basketball, they talk about that game on ESPN."

At one point, Brent hit eight straight three-point shots. "The announcer kept up with them at that point, and I could hear it on the sound system," Brent says, "so I knew right where I was."

Then he hit his ninth three-pointer.

"The record for three-point shots at the University of

Oklahoma is ten in one game," the announcer said. "One more and Price has tied the record. Two more and he breaks it."

Brent took his stance. Loyola was covering him close. "The guy was like glue," Brent says. Loyola was doing everything it could to cool him off, but that just wasn't going to happen that night—anyway, anyhow.

After his ninth three-pointer, Oklahoma brought the ball down and passed to Brent in the corner. "The guy was locked tight on me. I could barely move," he says. "I dribbled. I was a little off balance. I was as tight in the corner as you can be. Then I shot. I didn't think it could go in."

The crowd almost hushed as the ball sailed.

It struck the backboard. Banked.

And in!

Ten three-pointers. Brent Price had tied the record.

Now: Could he break it?

"People talk about that tenth shot. That's the one. But there was another one after it. And that broke the record." Final score: 172–112, U.O.

Brent barely remembers most of it. It was such an exciting night, he hardly believed he'd played the game till he saw it later on TV. He sank 11 three-pointers, going 11 for 20 attempts, 55 percent from three-point range, an excellent percentage. All told, he went 20 for 33, with 11 three-point shots, 18 regular points, and 5 free throws—56 points total. It was the third-highest score by a single player that year. He beat out Shaquille O'Neal's 53-point effort against Arkansas State and Kenny Anderson's 50 against the same Loyola team. Brent set several team and school records that day and began to look like an NBA contender, just like his brother.

The next year, Brent played in 30 games and scored 560 points with 185 assists. And the NBA made an offer. The Washington Bullets took him in the second round, thirty-second pick overall.

Brent's seasons with the Bullets have been a disappointment. Not because of the team, but because injuries have kept Brent from putting forth his best effort. Sitting on the sidelines in the 1994–95 season was tough.

"I learned a lot, though," Brent says. "I found myself discovering patience in a new way, and learning to trust in God's plan and his strength. That verse in Proverbs 3:5–6 helped. 'Trust in the Lord with all your heart and do not lean on your own understanding.' I had to do that plenty of times. I'm learning to trust, be patient, be positive."

One verse that has meant a lot to Brent in the past year is Colossians 3:23: "Whatever you do, work at it with all your heart, as working for the Lord." Brent says, "After that 56-point game I had other games that weren't nearly as good. Sometimes I was the hero. Sometimes I wasn't. I found out that trying to please everybody—my parents, friends, coach, and the media—was impossible.

"I had a Christian roommate who played football and he helped me, reminded me of Colossians 3:23. It helped me take my eyes off what I was doing and put them on the Lord. I realized it doesn't matter what others think, it matters what God thinks. So that's what I try to do with everything in life—please the Lord. Everything else doesn't matter."

Brent should have some fine years ahead of him. With an attitude like that, he will surely excel.

And maybe next time he plays against his brother, he'll outshoot, outdribble, and just generally outplay the guy!

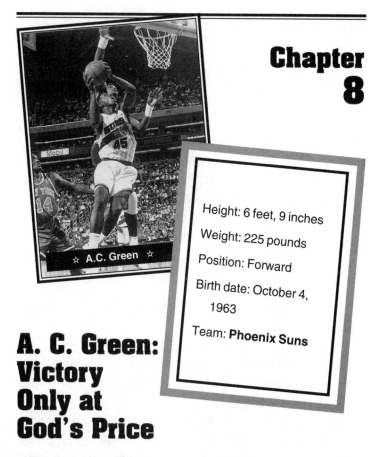

Height: 6 feet, 9 inches

Weight: 225 pounds

Position: Forward

Birth date: October 4, 1963

Team: **Phoenix Suns**

☆ A.C. Green ☆

A. C. Green: Victory Only at God's Price

The summer before his senior year in high school was the first time A. C. Green had ever flown on a plane. He had been invited to play in the Basketball Congress Invitational in Birmingham, Alabama.

The first night he and some friends walked toward the dorm. Suddenly, A. C. noticed something light up by his head. He swung at it, not knowing what it was. He sprinted a few yards, then cried out, "What's that chasing me?"

"Fireflies," one of the guys answered.

"What's that?"

"You know, lightning bugs," another guy answered. They didn't have lightning bugs like that in Oregon. A. C. had never seen such a thing before. At that moment, another one lit up right by A. C.'s ear. He galloped all the way to the safety of the dorm. The guys roared with laughter.

"You've never heard of fireflies?" one asked as he walked into the dorm. "They're bugs that light up at night."

"There are no bugs that light up!" A. C. insisted, completely rattled.[1]

It was the beginning of an education for A. C. Green. He realized that though he played some hot-shot basketball, he still remained ignorant of many marvels in the world.

A. C. grew up in a family with strong values and commitments. He looked up to his father and mother as his primary role models. They encouraged "Junior" all through school to work on his game and keep up his studies. At Benson High School in Portland, A. C. had an excellent opportunity to do just that. Coach Gray drove his boys, but he also produced winners. When A. C. started on the freshman team he was only five feet ten inches tall. By the next year he'd grown to six-three. His junior year he sprouted up to six-seven and finally in college he reached six feet eight and a half inches. Later, in the NBA, he would finish his growing years at just over six-nine.

A. C.'s best year in high school was undoubtedly his senior year. Early in the season, Benson played a rival, Hillsboro, which had two all-state players on its roster. Benson wanted blood.

Hillsboro won, though, by a few points in the last few seconds, much to Benson's disappointment.

After that, A. C.'s team fired up. During a game against their archrival, Grant, A. C. snagged a ball from an opponent at about three-quarters court. He dribbled toward the goal in a fast break, wanting to dunk the ball. But a Grant would-be hero cut him off about five feet from the basket.

A. C. stood there dribbling.

Suddenly, he palmed the ball as he'd seen Dr. J (Julius Erving) do on TV. He windmilled it from way back behind his head and leaped. Bringing his hand around with a slam, he pitched it down and through the basket.

Dunkeroo! Right through!

The crowd went crazy, and Benson went on to crush Grant.

Benson got a reputation that year for high scoring games. They averaged over 90 points for each 32-minute game. But when they came up against Wilson High School, the opposing coach advised his players to hold the ball. "Don't give it to Benson," he told them, and they played a slowdown, low scoring style. The game's turtle pace soon had the Wilson fans booing their own team. So in the fourth quarter, the Wilson coach told his players to go and play, to enjoy themselves. Forget slowing it down.

Benson came alive. They scored 56 points in that fourth quarter and won, 73–19. For A. C. it was the largest margin he had ever seen as a player. A. C. scored 40 points. In fact, A. C. averaged 29 points a game that season.

That year, Benson went to the championships, destroyed Grant in the first round, and mowed down the rest of the competition. In the final, they faced tough Hillsboro again, the team that had defeated them early in the season. Whoever won would take home the trophy and a busload of pride. A. C. hungered for that trophy.

A. C. started Benson off with two quick buckets, and after three minutes, Benson led, 10–4. By the half they were up by 10 points. With 2:56 to go in the last quarter, they steamed along 14 points ahead of Hillsboro.

Twelve thousand people crammed Memorial Coliseum. The noise deafened the players. Opposing bands struck up their school fight songs. It was pandemonium.

Everyone was shouting raucously, "We're number one!" A. C. and his team became totally distracted. They still had 2:56 to go.

And suddenly, Hillsboro came alive. In the next forty-five seconds, they stomped on Benson and cut the fourteen-point lead in half. Benson lost their momentum. It was as if the blood had just been sucked out of their bodies.

With a minute to go, they remained ahead by 6.

Hillsboro scored again.

Ahead by 4.

Then a Benson player dunked one. It was Greg "Doc" West. He stood five-eight, but he could jump!

He was also fouled, so that gave Benson another point.

Ahead by 7.

Finally, they reached the last ten seconds, and the crowd counted it down: "Ten, nine, eight . . ."

Suddenly, two Hillsboro shots put the enemy within 3.

What was happening? Benson was throwing it away!

"Seven, six, five . . ."

Another Hillsboro all-state player put it away for another 2 points.

Up by 1! Could Benson hold on?

"Three, two, one!"

Yes!

The place erupted. Benson had won—74–73—and took their place as state champs.

They went out with a 26–1 record that year. They were the team to beat! The *Oregonian* newspaper named A. C. to the 1981 all-metro team.

A. C. walked on air for a long time after that. But in the meantime, he had other things to consider—like college.

And something else.

A. C. had attended church much of his life. He felt as though he was okay with God, and God was okay with him. But he had no real relationship with Christ.

Then one weekend during the summer, Rod Bragano, one of A. C.'s teachers at Benson, and his wife, Karen, invited some of the guys up to their home in Hermiston, Oregon. Rod worked with the FCA (Fellowship of Christian Athletes) up there.

On Sunday, Rod invited the guys to attend church with him. Everything went as usual. A. C. wasn't even paying much attention until the preacher revved up in a message entitled, "Do You Want to Go to Heaven, or Do You Want to Go to Hell?"

As the pastor spelled out the gospel, A. C. found himself listening intently. And getting uncomfortable. He suddenly realized he was separated from God, lost, a sinner, and headed for hell.

God opened A. C.'s eyes that morning. He knew he needed Christ now, for salvation, for hope, for life.

Until that point in his life, A. C. was your basic people pleaser. Whatever others wanted to do, he did. Thus, at the moment when the pastor gave an altar call, Satan jumped in with some people-pleasing lines of false wisdom.

"Let someone else go first," a little voice told A.C. "They're going to laugh at you if you go first."

A. C. felt the blood draining from his face. No one was moving. Was he going to do this all alone?

Moments sped by as the pastor asked for the third time if anyone wanted to come forward.

It was now or never. A. C. pushed past Ricky Stewart, who was sitting at the end of the pew, and went forward.

Once there, the pastor asked him, "Do you know what you're doing, son?"

"No, I don't," A. C. replied.

The pastor stepped down and talked and prayed with him for a few minutes until A. C. did understand. Then the pastor asked him to turn around.

One more time, Satan's voice filled A. C.'s head.

"All your friends are going to laugh at you."

"They're gonna call you stupid."

"They won't talk to you now."

But none of that happened. Instead, the whole church clapped and cheered.

It was the beginning of A. C.'s walk with Christ. And it thrust into his mind a powerful lesson: "All the devil's lines are lies. Don't listen to him."[2]

Next on the agenda for A. C. was Oregon State University, OSU, where he hoped to make his mark as someone who might play in the NBA.

In college, A. C. played forward most of the time. He had played center in high school, but that was over now. Power forward became his position. His junior year he was named Pac-10 player of the year. He also captured fourth in the nation in shooting percentage (.667). He set OSU per-game records in scoring (17.5) and rebounds (8.5).

His last year on the team at OSU turned out to be his best. AP (Associated Press) and UPI (United Press International) selected him as third-team all-American and he gained a spot on the all-Pac-10 team for the third year in a row. He was also Region 8 player of the year. OSU named him most valuable player for the second time; he led the team in scoring (19.1 per game), steals, and rebounding (9.2 per game). That year he also scored a career-high 39 points against Stanford. The honors and accomplishments capped his four years of basketball at OSU.

Now it was NBA time. A. C. nervously waited to see what would happen with the NBA draft. Plenty of teams came to look: Philadelphia, Portland, Boston, Denver, Los Angeles. But he didn't know who would take him. And he didn't know whether he would even be selected in the first or second round.

It was a hair-raising moment.

A. C. and his family sat in a hotel awaiting the results. Then at 11:52 A.M. Los Angeles took their pick. "A. C. Green out of Oregon State U." Number twenty-three. In the first round.

When a reporter asked him how he felt, he said, "I thank God. I just thank God."

The NBA was an all-new experience for A. C. The Lakers' style of play was extraordinary, and they called it "Showtime." It was definitely a show. Run, shoot, rebound, dunk. That was the name of the game. A. C. would play right alongside Kareem Abdul-Jabbar, Magic Johnson, and James Worthy. The greats!

Could he compete?

Time would tell. But very soon he knew. He could. That first year, he averaged 6.4 points per game, and he played in all 82 games of the regular season.

But it was his second year that stood in the spotlight.

The finals. Boston against Los Angeles. The old rivalry between two basketball dynasties. Celtics and Lakers. Robert Parish, Kevin McHale, Larry Bird—names that go down in history. A. C. would go up against them.

The Lakers had blown through the championships like a ship with a hurricane tail wind. But it was the big Celtics who stood in the way of a championship. They played the first game in Boston, beating the Celtics, 126–113, even though Larry Bird cashed his first eleven shots in a row.

The second game was a repeat: L.A. snuffed them, 141–122. It was looking like a rout.

Then in the third game on Laker home turf at the Forum, the Lakers flattened out, losing, 109–103. Coach Riley blustered up and down on the sidelines the whole game, but nothing could get the Lakers to catch fire.

In the locker room, Riley yelled, "None of you has given 100 percent."

Riley chewed them out, then called on A. C. for a word. A. C. told them, "We can't be full of pride. If the team becomes full of pride, we could get ahead of ourselves and lose." He felt it was a word from God for the team.

The Lakers went out and played hard ball against the Celtics in game four. It was a tough game, contested right down to the end. With two seconds to go, the Celtics led by 1 point, but it was the Lakers' ball. The ball was inbounded to Magic Johnson. He drove down the lane and skyhooked the ball Kareem-style, a shot he'd never taken before. It whisked through and the Lakers won, 107–106. The crowd went wild. 3–1. It looked like a Lakers rout for sure!

The Lakers had won in 1985 this way. Could it be a repeat?

The Celtics, though, came out in game five loaded for baskets. They took the Lakers down, 123–108. Game score, 3–2, Lakers.

The team returned to Boston Garden for game six, Celtic turf. It would be a tough battle. The Celtics led 56–51 at the half.

But two minutes into the third quarter, James Worthy made a play that will go down in basketball history. He stole the ball from Kevin McHale, then chased it down the sidelines. At the last second, he dove and grabbed the ball just before it went out. He hefted it to Magic Johnson, already on a fast break. Magic dunked it. The Lakers led, 57–56.

That third quarter was basketball magic. The Lakers outscored, outshot, outrebounded, and out-dribbled the Celtics 30 points to 12. At the buzzer, it was 106–93. The Lakers had won, and A. C. celebrated like he never had before. This was one from the Lord.

In his eight seasons with the Lakers, A. C. regularly scored over 10 points a game with over 7 rebounds. He was traded to the Phoenix Suns, where he continues a tradition of faith, hope, and love with his fellow Christians there, Kevin Johnson, Wayman Tisdale, and the coach, Paul Westphal.

Undoubtedly, he'll continue to make his mark on and off the court. With his special project in L.A., A. C. Green's Programs for Youth, A. C. has become a more and more powerful spokesman for strong

Christian values, sexual abstinence until marriage, and increasing math and reading skills.

He's a person to look up to, not just because of his height on the basketball court, but because of his walk in the court of life.

---

1. Story adapted from A. C. Green with J. C. Webster, *Victory* (Lake Mary, Fla.: Creation House, 1994), 37.
2. Story adapted from *Victory*, 45–46.

Don't miss out on the other books in the Sports Heroes series!

Sports Heroes: Baseball
0-310-49551-2
$4.99
Smashing a winning home run in the ninth inning of a World Series game. Baseball fans dream of it. Joe Carter has done it. Find out what it's like in *Sports Heroes: Baseball*. Plus, meet Orel Hershiser, who pitched 59 consecutive no-run innings—and other great players who share with you the excitement, challenges, and secrets of becoming a major-league star.

Sports Heroes: Basketball
0-310-49561-X
$4.99
Take to the court with some of the NBA's best players. This action-packed book puts you right in the game! Score almost at will with Mark Price's offensive power. Bury opponents with the deadly three-point accuracy of Hersey Hawkins. And find out what some of the greatest stars do *off* the court as well as on it. Here's a thorough look at what it takes to make it in basketball today.

Sports Heroes: Football
0-310-49571-7
$4.99
Go head-to-head with some of the greatest players and coaches in the NFL. *Sports Heroes: Football* will let you taste last-minute victory through Roger Staubach's famous two-minute offense, take you on-field with defensive giant Reggie White, and show you the ins and outs of NFL stardom through the eyes of some of football's biggest stars.

Sports Heroes: Track and Field
0-310-49581-4
$4.99
What would it be like to race world-record-setter Carl Lewis—and win? Leroy Burrell, the runner who beat Lewis to become the fastest man in the world, can tell you. He's just one of the champions you'll meet in *Sports Heroes: Track and Field*—heroes like decathlete Dave Johnson, who won an Olympic medal despite a broken foot. Find out from them what it takes to reach the Olympics in track and field.